You Know You're a
Sailing Fanatic
When...

Ben Fraser

summersdale

YOU KNOW YOU'RE A SAILING FANATIC WHEN...

Summersdale Publishers Ltd
46 West Street
Chichester
West Sussex
PO19 1RP
UK

www.summersdale.com

Printed and bound in China

ISBN: 978-1-84953-072-9

Substantial discounts on bulk quantities of Summersdale books are available to corporations, professional associations and other organisations. For details contact Summersdale Publishers by telephone: +44 (0) 1243 771107, fax: +44 (0) 1243 786300 or email: nicky@summersdale.com.

You Know You're a
Sailing Fanatic
When...

On long car journeys you forego satnav for a sextant and a compass.

You ask for permission to 'come alongside' every time you climb into bed with your partner.

The ringtone on your mobile is the theme from *Howard's Way*.

While getting dressed you can't help but experiment with knots.

You have your yacht club down as who
should be contacted in case
of emergencies.

You think something is 'a load of old rowlocks'.

You have toe straps fitted to your sofa so you can 'sit out' whilst watching TV.

You stop thinking of a cat as a
four-legged, furry animal.

A 'snubber' isn't just a snooty society hostess.

You get up in the middle of the night
and sleepily pee over the banister.

You don't understand why you are being given the eye by the local dominatrix after discussing a rigging screw.

You record the shipping forecast and listen to it repeatedly on your iPod.

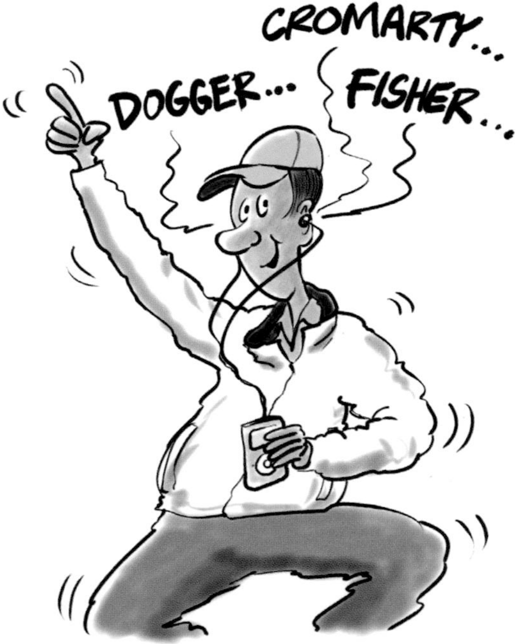
CROMARTY...
DOGGER...
FISHER...

The first thing you check on waking up
in the morning is the strength of
the wind.

You display your bitts without hint
of embarrassment.

You name your house 'Dundrifting'.

You can identify a bottlescrew, and know that its primary function isn't pulling out corks.

You shout 'Starboard!' on slip roads.

You realise that a seacock isn't an amphibious chicken.

You say 'over' at the end of every
sentence in telephone conversations.

You ask your mechanic if he can fit your car with a tiller rather than a wheel.

You have no qualms about rolling
around on a Galway Hooker.

Your loose talk won't scandalise
the mainsail.

Your partner sends you out to your local Spar shop and is surprised when you come back with a spinnaker pole.

You claim your favourite films are
Dances with Waves and *The Incredible
Hull*, while your favourite song is
'Hey Big Fender'.

A 'steaming light' doesn't just mean
the bulb is overheating.

You wouldn't have a tender behind if
you hadn't hooked up with the painter.

Whilst other children have bad dreams about ghosts and monsters, your kids worry about seeing the *Flying Dutchman.*

You don't need scales to weigh anchor.

You discover that breast ropes are not
a type of heavy-duty bra.

You don't get offended after someone comments on your baggywrinkles.

You find out that a 'long fetch' doesn't
mean throwing the dog's ball as far
as you can.

You'd like to haul a Yankee up the forestay.

An echo sounder doesn't refer to the torment inflicted by an exuberant Swiss yodeller.

You always need another pint at the bitter end.

'Tumblehome' doesn't just mean staggering back from the pub.

Thinking of Cowes Week as an agricultural show is a load of old bull.

You don't wince at the excruciating
thought of ground tackle.

Your wife insists on a divorce after she overhears you talking about cruising for lost buoys.

You have a scale model of the *Cutty Sark* to play with in the bath.

You have red and green lights to guide
you into your garage and rig fenders
on your car before attempting
the manoeuvre.

You have no fear of sinking just
because you're in irons.

Your visit to a Yankee Clipper doesn't
result in an American-style short back
and sides.

You wonder why Texans are always talking about yawls.

Your wife is growing tired of you serenading her with endless sea shanties accompanied on the accordion.

You've just lost a race and yet feel no
compulsion to throw knives at
your daggerboard.

You give the distance in cables every time you're asked for directions.

You've taught the kids to lean out
over the sides of the car as you drive
around corners.

Being 'off soundings' is in no way
related to your aversion to flatulence.

You wonder whether a parrot, an eye-patch and an amputation would add to your personal image.

You try to pump water into the kitchen
sink at home with your foot.

Your idea of a sailmaker's palm is one that is neither crossed with silver nor one that slaps you across the face.

'Painting her bottom' isn't only
something for consenting adults.

You can talk about a 'gooseneck'
without sniggering.

You're sent out to buy sheets and come back with a selection of sails for your experimental five-sail Bermuda rig.

You get a written warning at work for attempting to gain your boss's attention by shouting 'Ahoy!' across the office.

The phrase 'sacrificial strip' doesn't prompt you to streak for charity.

Your friend has bought you some Velcro shoes because they're fed up with constantly cutting you free from complicated shoelace knots.

You christen your children by aiming a bottle of champagne at their rears.

You've caught a roach in
your mainsail.

Your concerned neighbours decide to call Animal Welfare after they overhear you talking about your dolphin striker.

The first and last time your wife asked you to help out with housework you bleached the dining table with teak brightener.

A gaff-rigged boat isn't the result of an embarrassing error.

You think telltales are good to
have around.

Your partner is tired of you saying 'you float my boat' and still laughing after the five-hundredth time.

You don't feel any better after you've been overhauled.

The double glazing men turn up and you request that they fit portholes to your house.

You totally get the wrong end of the stick after being asked to give your misbehaving child a stern line or two.

The cry 'All hands on deck!' doesn't mean you are about to do press-ups.

Getting your dinghy on the plane has nothing to do with paying for excess baggage.

'Aloft' isn't just another word for attic.

You name your dogs Bowsprit and Bobstay and their baskets are known as the 'crew quarters'.

You wish you had a crow's nest on the top of your house so that you could scan the horizon for marauding pirates.

Have you enjoyed this book?
If so, why not write a review
on your favourite website?

Thanks very much for buying
this Summersdale book.

www.summersdale.com